*Workforce Champion:*

# Breaking Through

# Workforce Champion:

# Breaking Through

*Imagine Better & The Principle of Growth*

LaTonya Darneish McElroy, MBA, SPHR, SHRM-SCP/TA

*Cover image:* Tyrone Dodson Photographer, Texarkana, TX

*Cover design:* Byron Walker, Texarkana, TX

# Dedication

Workforce Champion: Breaking Through is dedicated to many developing workforce champions who are striving to work faithfully, daily, and who are on the verge of going to their next level, if only they can believe, unlock their potential, overcome the limitations and pressure, and break through.

# Table of Contents

# Introduction

The Workforce Champion Series is the result of a real-life journey through each of these principles, which carried me from failure, setbacks and under-employment, to success, multiple promotions, and enough income to create a comfortable life for our family, with peace and the satisfaction of knowing I got here honestly.

If you commit to following these eight principles, you can prepare yourself for new opportunities and promotion.

You can be ready when your next opportunity presents itself. Take advantage of these principles. Prepare to meet your destiny and to gain your credentials of character, paving the way to achieve your next level of success and influence.

This series, Workforce Champion, provides you the opportunity to gain your credentials of workforce character, to certify that you have completed a program of study and a journey of self-development, in preparation for your next promotion, your new job or your new opportunity. I promise, if you are following these principles, greater is coming.

*Disclaimer: This book is written from a Christian worldview. The ideas and beliefs are not intended to represent those of anyone besides the author and do not take away from the principles shared herein, but are used as a fundamental basis for thought, belief, and self-view.*

# Chapter 1

Breaking Through: The Principle of Growth

The pressure is mounting, you feel like you are about to explode, and you cannot see the light of day. …and guess what? You're exactly where you need to be. It's time for you to break through. It's time for the next level of growth. Growth is not a theory. Growth is a principle. When the force on the inside of you becomes strong enough to equal and then exceed the negative or natural pressures from outside of you, growth… just… happens. It is important to understand that growth is <u>not</u> a theory, as in simply a hypothetical or a *maybe*. Growth is not something that is abstract. Growth is a process. It is a principle, and it will work for you. So, the goal in our preparation program is to get you ready, to grow you, to get you in line for the opportunities that are about to come your way.

If you are growing on the inside you will see growth on the outside. When a fetus grows, the mother's womb expands. When a plant grows, it spreads and climbs. When a person grows, the shoe and clothing sizes change. And when we develop internally, our influence enlarges, and we are capable of handling greater assignments.

When are you ready to be promoted? It is when preparation meets opportunity. It is when you have *grown*. Growth is not a figment of our imagination. Growth can be observed with the natural eye. Growth can be felt. Growth is both tangible and inevitable when the right principles are at work on the inside.

What is on the inside of you? I want to challenge you, your inner and greater *you*, to break out. What if your current state is only the seed of what you are becoming. Think about that. Though your current state may seem ugly, not feel attractive, look small, have rough edges, and not appear as you think it should in order to achieve the outcome you are expecting. What if we make it look good, but we're only dressing up the *seed* of who we are? Maybe you do not *look the part* that you envision for yourself, and in reality, you are just where you need to be. As much as we dress up the external, until we break through, we are existing far from our potential? What if what we will become is so much greater than what we see and are right now? What if?

To further elaborate on the concept of the seed, consider a pear or an apple seed. The seed often has a gruesome appearance. It looks nothing like the actual tree or the fruit. It does not have a delicious taste, and the outward appearance is certainly not attractive. An onlooker from the outside (looking in) would not look at that seed and say 'oh that's a peach or pear tree.' However, what if our destiny is so great that it looks nothing like what we look like right now? What if your end destination bears no resemblance whatsoever to where you are right now?

Let's ask ourselves a series of questions to help us determine how to break through. How do we activate the principle of growth to create the full, abundant life we have always wanted? Are you ready to take this journey with me?

## Champion's Journey - Chapter 1 Worksheet

| |
|---|
| Key takeaway: |
| Goal(s): |
| What will I stop? |
| What will I minimize? |
| What will I keep doing? |
| What will I do more of? |
| What will I start? |
| What is my timeline / deadline? |
| With what person(s) will I share these commitments? |

# Chapter 2

## Can You Imagine Greater?

I want to challenge you not to think only of your surroundings as in your place of employment, the building or the company, your home or your relationships. I want you to think outside of those types of things, because I have discovered that none of those things truly define you, and none of those things truly can *con*fine you.

The challenge is to realize that our current circumstances may present physical restraints, and they may cause us to feel trapped, confined, or frustrated, but our feelings in these moments do not actually matter, our emotions do not matter, and sometimes even our environment and what it looks like does not matter. Here is the reality: there is another perspective. There is a better view. Maybe those things that feel like traps and barriers are not truly confining us or holding us back at all. Could it be that those pressures and constraints are necessary, like the dirt covering a seed, which is actually providing the nurturing and the pressure needed for us to break out? So, these elements may be confining our mentality. They may be limiting our vision. But they do not define who we are or how far we can go. Ultimately, what defines us and determines our journey is what is at work on the inside.

Let us take a moment to think and evaluate. What if where you are in terms of your mentality or vision is too small? What if your belief or your imagination is not large or expansive enough?

We often use the phrases 'I believe' and 'I have faith.' My question is, 'faith in what?' Some of us have faith in God. That's not only our belief that He exists, but also faith to believe that God loves us and is our greatest source above our jobs, our relationships, and our own abilities. Many of us believe our faith in God is ultimately what sustains us. However, I want to ask 'what do you believe about yourself?'

Let's reach back into our childhoods for a state of mind that is the incubator for what we believe. We will have to travel over the obstacles of adulthood, past the shattered dreams of teenage-dom, and into the lost and almost forgotten spaces of a time when we best used our *imagination*. The word *imagination* makes me think about a scripture that might be familiar and which says, 'I am able to do exceeding abundantly above all that you can ask or think. (Olive Tree)' Just what *can* you ask or think? What can you dream up in your imagination? What can you see with your mind's eye, without seeing it first with the human eye? *That* is your imagination.

This passage gives clues that God is, in fact, encouraging us to ask and to *think*. He says 'I am able to do ABOVE even that' and thinking involves using the framework of knowledge and past experiences – climbing that ladder of assurance. Each step is built off of the known reality. Activating our imagination is like climbing that ladder and then standing at the very, tip-top – then building the next prongs with our own two hands. This is where 'above what we think' lives – in our imagination. With our imaginations we activate the process and build a framework for what we can believe is possible.

The first step to getting beyond our present circumstances is to change our state of mind. We cannot be blinded by our circumstances, but instead we must exercise our ability to imagine greater – to see with our minds' eye beyond the present. If where we are is too small, we must begin to imagine greater, until we are convinced that although what we see may appear impossible, what we *imagine* is possible if we can believe.

A few years ago, I began packing our least-used belongings (dishes, clothing, decorations) in boxes, to my husband's raised brows. We even began having small updates/renovations done to our home, because I had seen a glimpse of where we were going, although only with the eyes of my imagination. In my imagination, one morning, I saw the vaulted ceiling in the new bedroom as I threw my legs out of bed, and I was almost out of breath when I repeated the vision to everyone in the house. At this point, while seeing and feeling the change taking place in my mind, nothing about our circumstances pointed towards a new home, not even as a remote possibility. Yet, a new home was what I saw. I imagined it, and I began to believe it so deeply that I started preparing. During this period, visitors would come by our home and ask about the boxes. Of course, I would tell them, 'we're moving.' But the next question was always, 'oh, where are you moving to?' to which my response was always, 'I'm not sure yet,' with an unbothered smile.

Fast-forwarding to now, it has been several years since we began living in the 'imagined' home with the vaulted ceiling in the bedroom. The truth – the home was only the destination. The journey of opening my imagination to greater possibilities was my greatest gain. This same principle applies to every aspect of life.

So, I want you to ask yourself and consider for just a moment. Are you able to imagine greater? Are you able to imagine exponentially greater than where you are today? If not, what is hindering you?

Has someone told you it is not okay to dream? Has someone told you it is not okay to have an imagination anymore?

### 

*"You're not a child anymore. Therefore, you must set aside all of these childish dreams and ambitions… those radical ideas are not going to actually come to pass. What happens to 'them,' as in other people, is only a rare occurrence, 'one in a million shot.'"*

### 

Has someone told you it is no longer okay to dream, to imagine, to think outside of where you are? Has someone told you that?

If so, I want you to go through this mental process with me. This process is a good exercise to help clean-up and detoxify your thoughts. Coincidentally, when the body needs to eliminate wastes by means including natural excretion or digestion, we call that process detoxifying (or detoxing). There are waves and herds of items to buy to assist our bodies with the detox process, from diets, to teas and colon cleanses. Well, recent research by two US researchers was submitted for peer review to the Department of Health and Human Services, and their study demonstrates that the brain's matter also has a detoxifying system that's just being discovered, which removes protein buildup that's believed to be a main contributing factor for degenerative aging issues, Alzheimer's and Parkinson's.

"In our research, we found an undiscovered system for clearing proteins and other wastes from the brain—and learned that this system is most active during sleep. The need to remove potentially toxic wastes from the brain may, in fact, help explain the mystery of why we sleep and hence retreat from wakefulness for a third of our lives. We fully expect that an understanding of what happens when this system malfunctions will lead us to both new diagnostic techniques and treatments for a host of neurological illnesses." (Netergaard et al.)

The physical brain needs cleansing!

So, what about our thoughts? What is it called when we cleanse our thoughts – the words we rehearse in our minds over and over? The University of Wisconsin Health simply calls it "thought-stopping." It's pretty simple. You list your most stressful thoughts, imagine the thought, and then stop it! Do this however it works for you.

Here is an exercise you might try with me: Take the negativity towards your dreams, those downing conversations, and those dream-killing, imagination-destroying thoughts that have replayed in your mind – even the tone and the *very* sound of them, the voices of the people who have said them, and even your own voice. I want you to, for a moment, paint all of those voices and words on an imaginary canvas, and I want you to make it vivid with all of the color and ugliness you felt when you listened to those words.

Why do I want you to paint an imaginary canvas of those thoughts? Because I want you to look at them ONE LAST TIME. After today, we're not looking at our limitations and what people have told us that we cannot be, but instead, we are destroying that canvas. I know you have become attached to these thoughts. I know they tell an ironically beautiful story. I know you've been looking at them and hearing them for years. I know you *thought* you had to accept this limiting self-image and accept as truth these hurtful words, trying to come to terms with them, believing they may be true about you. But, they are NOT.

As with abstract art, the artist's expression is their view of beauty and may be highly popularized or respected. However, not everyone can or will agree. Something that may even be of very little material value is suddenly worth millions, based on the observer's perspective. I have seen some pretty incredible abstract art, with creative meaning and a message that resonates. However, there have been times when I was not so impressed, such as when I lied on the floor of a paid exhibit, staring up into a duct tape, garbage bag and cellophane ceiling. I'm sure the artist created it with some purpose in mind—a meaning that I did not grasp. However, not everyone can or will appreciate his artistry, while others will idolize it. That admiration is how we sometimes idolize and overvalue the words that have been spoken over our lives, and oftentimes the value of those spoken words are simply a matter of perspective.

It does not matter *who* has spoken the limits over us. I apologize on their behalf. I am sorry that mama or daddy said it. I am sorry that a grandmother or grandfather said those words. I am sorry that the mentor, boss or someone that you looked up to said it. I am sorry that you have even looked at yourself in the mirror and even told yourself these negative things.

I am sorry about the limits that have been placed on your imagination, but today is a burial date for that picture. Today is a burial date for that memorial, that image that has constantly haunted your thoughts and constantly snatched your imagination from you. I want you, today, to destroy it. Mentally go through the exercise of destruction of those words. Do not ever bring them out again. In fact, just burn this canvas out of your mind. Destroy it in such a way that it can never be reassembled, because those things are holding you back, and today, you will unleash your imagination over yourself.

We realize the importance of being guided in our imaginations (being realistic and not simply whimsical), but I want to challenge you with this belief: *If we can imagine greater than where we are… if we can simply imagine greater, we put a force on the inside of us that puts pressure on our outer shell (what we and others see). It puts internal force on the inside --to give us the power to begin to break through.*

Remember the scripture that states 'according to the power that works on the inside of us?'… in some cases this is God-given power and potential. The imagination is your God-given and God-connected creative domain – the area that makes you much like God and the area where you can generate inspired thoughts and ideas. God has given you the power of your imagination to create, just as He creates. How will you use it? On the inside, you have the power to create, imagine, or even re-imagine your future.

As a result, if you can exercise the power to create something greater than where you are, you can begin the construction phase – to physically bring what you imagined into time and space. Though the final destination (where you actually end up) may not perfectly match what you first imagined, what that imagination does for you is two things:

1) Your imagined future allows you to stretch beyond where you are, in the direction of your imagination.

2) Your imagined future allows you to mentally explore other opportunities and other options for your life – options you may not explore if only focused on what you can see today.

With stretching and exploring, you may find that you no longer desire the future you originally imagined, but at least at that point you have stretched beyond your current level of existence and seen something greater. Now, you are further than you *were*, maybe not going in the *exact* direction you need or want to go, but like a plane that is slightly off-course, you can adjust and realign your imagination. You are flying now! Your imagination is not a permanent fixture. The best thing about imagination is it can be redirected and recreated, but it cannot be stopped unless *you* allow it. Imagine greater!

| |
|---|
| Key takeaway: |
| Goal(s): |
| What will I stop? |
| What will I minimize? |
| What will I keep doing? |
| What will I do more of? |
| What will I start? |
| What is my timeline / deadline? |
| With what person(s) will I share these commitments? |

# Chapter 3

Are you willing to make adjustments?

Have you ever written a note by hand, and as you were writing it, you misspelled something or you wrote a wrong letter, and you thought, "instead of starting over, I think I'll just turn that accidental 'r' into an 'e'." For another example, can you recall a time when you were headed for a particular destination, and GPS recalculated your route to accommodate or adjust for a wrong turn or traffic delays?

This is what your imagination allows you to do. Put an imaginary brush to the canvas of your mind and begin to paint your life. Then, as you paint, if you arrive at the need to change your angle or make corrections, you have the artistic privilege to paint something new. That is what we call adjusting.

When you create your own destiny, YOU are the one with the instrument in hand. You are the one imagining your future. The outcome of your life begins in your imagination, and therefore, once you begin to paint the picture, it is up to you to make necessary adjustments. Life will happen. Things will not always go as planned. We will run into obstacles. People and circumstances will change. We have to be able to adjust to both the unexpected and expected changes of life.

Much like a canvas, if we accidentally slip or pick the wrong color, we can improvise or re-imagine our next season. We can change that accidental into a new image on our canvas or mix in another color to transform it to something new. So it is with life. Maybe we end up slightly off schedule or in another direction than our original aim. What will we do if we have worked hard, pressed ahead, and we do not end up exactly where we planned? I want you to understand that imagination does not lock you into your destination, but imagination gives you the power and the force to look beyond where you are. Turn around and look behind you. *Maybe* you are not where you thought you would be, but look how far you have come. Maybe you are not where you *want* to be, but you are not where you were. Keep imagining!

I found an article that sums this up:

### 

*"Imagination is the key to success, since everything you create, build or achieve begins in the imagination... Every ambition, goal and plan starts in the mind, in the imagination, and only later turns into reality... Your imagination is responsible, largely, for your current life circumstances, and it also affects your future, because what you are imagining now in your mind will be what you would experience tomorrow and in the future... Imagination is the rehearsal room, where you rehearse in your mind what you want to do or accomplish. It is a way to eliminate mistakes and errors and save time when you actually proceed with your action." (Sasson)*

### 

Now, I want you to imagine 'greater,' and when necessary, make adjustments.

| Key takeaway: |
| --- |
| Goal(s): |
| What will I stop? |
| What will I minimize? |
| What will I keep doing? |
| What will I do more of? |
| What will I start? |
| What is my timeline / deadline? |
| With what person(s) will I share these commitments? |

# Chapter 4

Is your capacity and willingness to learn constraining you? Is your glass already full? What is your power level?

I know that we, in general, are educated—some having degrees and certificates, licenses and letters behind our names, courses and college hours on our transcripts, and maybe even a number of books on our kindles or shelves. However, our challenge is realizing that no matter how much knowledge we have gained, there is always more–more to understand, more to truly learn. Acquired knowledge is only a droplet in the universe of available knowledge, awaiting our exploration and understanding. So, what do we do? Do we give up on learning? No! We go fiercely after knowledge, we hunger for it, we strive to gain all the knowledge we can!

Even in doing so, we can *never* completely explore all there is to be known. We also want to avoid gaining mere knowledge without understanding. So, at this point, let us commit to gaining knowledge and learning for an entire lifetime. There is not a moment in your career, in your family life, in your relationships, in your faith, in any walk or avenue of your life where you will have arrived at your ultimate capacity to learn or understand. In fact, knowledge is potential. If we can grasp more knowledge, we can increase our potential. Just imagine what can happen if we focus that knowledge in areas where we have imagined ourselves going. We can achieve great things!

What causes people to stop learning? Do they feel they have already arrived, that they know all there is to know in an area? Is their glass so full that nothing else can be poured into it? As the saying goes, you cannot pour from an empty cup, and you can not fill an already full glass. Lolly Daskal gives four reasons: 1) They know what they know, 2) They know what they do not know, 3) They do not know what *is* known, and 4) They do not know the unknown.

I can translate that: 1) They have limited their own knowledge with closed mindedness, 2) They think they know it all, 3) They have no clue how much more knowledge is already at their fingertips and been discovered, and 4) They have no idea how much more knowledge (through research and science) can be uncovered – that is not already known to man.

We should not allow ourselves to be either the empty cup, or the full glass. We want to be ever-gaining knowledge, because knowledge can be 'power.'

What do you know about the word 'potential' as it relates to energy? Did you know that *potential* energy is a form of energy that has not yet been transformed into *kinetic* / active energy? So, any object that has *potential* energy but lacks *kinetic* / active energy, is sitting still. It is *full* of potential and going nowhere.

However, an object that has transformed its potential energy into kinetic / active energy is an object that has now become a true force. So, it is vital to understand that gaining the right knowledge stores up our potential.

Our minds are like vehicles with a certain cylinder engine (cars usually come with four-, six- or eight-cylinder engines). The higher the cylinder, the more power is generated in a shorter amount of time. Higher cylinders usually mean better power and better performance. Who would not want that higher performance? The mind is our engine, and one of the main ways we increase our capacity for power and performance is by gaining more knowledge. That knowledge gives us the potential to do great things.

Knowledge is *potential* power. The greater the potential we have, the greater the power and performance we can demonstrate upon engagement. If you can fill your mind with the right knowledge, then you can be better prepared to perform at a higher level and achieve goals faster when the time comes.

If you are waiting on the opportunity, the open door, or the offer before you prepare, then you will have limited your impact and created barriers to your own success, because you have limited your own power. It is like a car that sells as a high-performance model but disappoints when you look under the hood, because it has a small, low-performance engine.

I challenge you to surprise your future opportunities in a good way! Be more than ready when the chance comes. Under-sell and overdeliver. Be equipped with the knowledge you need to have the greatest impact.

With the right knowledge, you have greater impact because you have stored up greater power. You are committed to learning more each day, and you are not afraid of a challenge. You are better today than you were yesterday, because you know more today than you knew yesterday. You are a force! You will conquer impossibilities because you are fully equipping your mind and ever-growing. You are a glass that is *never* empty and *never* full. The more you know, the more you grow.

A wise woman was in her seventies when she challenged me (tapping her finger on her temple) to 'get something up there that nobody can take away', and she meant to get knowledge! This seventy-something lady was my late, beloved grandmother ("Granny"), and she had been the first in her family to push beyond field labor and pursue her education to the end –

graduating from high school with a final graduation speech, a moment so cherished that she often recited parts of her graduation speech to her children and grandchildren.

Is knowledge power? Some say 'no.' I say, 'yes, knowledge is power,' but it is only *potential* power. True power is created when our potential is transformed into action and opportunity.'

The real question is, when opportunity comes, 'will you be ready to activate your power?'

| Key takeaway: |
| --- |
| Goal(s): |
| What will I stop? |
| What will I minimize? |
| What will I keep doing? |
| What will I do more of? |
| What will I start? |
| What is my timeline / deadline? |
| With what person(s) will I share these commitments? |

# Chapter 5

Are you in need of healing and restoration?

I want to take a moment to speak to those who have been in the workforce and have endured workforce hurt. This may be as a result of unreasonable oppression by a supervisor or a person in leadership. It could be your own sense of insufficiency in comparison to others. Maybe you have not been granted or offered opportunities, being unfairly overlooked. As a result, the pain has caused you to draw back from your dreams and the things that you have imagined yourself to accomplish and be. There could be a multitude of other examples of workforce hurt, even those not named here.

In this moment, still yourself and allow God to minister to your heart and spirit. Do you know He can heal and restore? Right now, let us not only talk about how you *should* feel, or tell you to 'shake it off' and 'get over it,' but instead let us face the offense, the hurt, and the pain – the sore, unhealed places. Let us pray that the oil (love, care and compassion) of God would begin to flow. 'Lord, we know that you are our healer. And we know that You mend broken pieces. You know the hurt that has been endured. You even know the secret lies and the manipulations. You know, Lord, the times when a person has smiled while their heart was hurting, the times when they endured a conversation and were being spoken down to or treated as if they were nothing, but they had to endure it for the sake of a paycheck and because they were thinking about their families. I thank you God for your healing and power to undo and restore every broken piece and every hurting, wounded heart.'

'Father, in the name of Jesus Christ, we ask that you restore their vision, restore their imagination, remove the smudges, and even heal the wounds so that they are whole and in no more pain. We ask that you would heal the wounds to the point that they are as if no hurt was ever there. Make them whole, leaving nothing – except maybe the scar or memory of the healing itself, to remind them just how far you have brought them. In the name of Jesus, I thank you that in this moment you are causing the healing to take place. In the future I pray that you would recover and restore them in such a way that no weapon or strategy against them will succeed. I also pray that you would not allow contrary words or disparaging statements to deter or hinder their success.'

'I thank you for touching the person reading and hearing this message. I pray that you would empower them with a force, a strength, and a tenacity that no evil person, thing, or thought can shake them – let there be a force on the inside that can resist and exceed any negative influence, words and actions. Thank You for being a restorer. I thank you that you are not only a restorer, but you give back in multiples, two and even ten times recovery of any losses. I thank you that losses caused by burdens and hardships, losses as a result of obstacles that were placed in their way, losses as a result of the constraints that were placed upon them, and losses caused by the real or perceived ceilings and walls that surrounded them, would be restored. I pray for restoration to even greater heights than that which they might have accomplished had they not been hindered. In the name of Jesus.'

'And as we pray, we ask for those who were the perpetrators and who trespassed against us, who even *caused* these hurts (spoke the negative words and put barriers in the way). Father, you know their hearts and do not desire for them to suffer. That is why we pray for restoration for that person. Heal them in the area that has caused them to do wrong toward others, and as they ask forgiveness from you, may they also repay their debtors. May they give back or pay it forward. They may not be able to undo what they have done, but in their future, let them run into opportunities to help or lend a helping hand— to somehow serve You better in their business or in their career, in the name of Jesus.'

'We thank you for the restoration, and we know it is only by your grace, Jesus, that we made it this far. It is only by Your grace that we accomplish dreams in spite of everything, and we know your grace will lead us on to greater heights and deeper depths—that greater horizons are on the way. We thank you in this moment for the preparation that is taking place in Jesus' name.'

If you agree with this prayer, it is my belief that you should express that agreement. Whether you say 'I agree' or 'Amen,' I hope that you have joined your faith with mine for total restoration.

As a personal life story to support this occurring, I had a difficult season of life and career setbacks. All of the above hurts were my true reality during this time. I thought that I would not be able to endure it. Yet, during this time, I prayed very similar prayers (not all at once). At first, I especially was unable to pray for the offenders. However, I felt inspired to journal my prayers. I would read scriptures and see how God restored others who had suffered. He always seemed to give them much more than they had lost. I began hoping for double of everything that I had lost. Because I wrote them down, I was absolutely blown away as each inconceivable wish came true.

Since that life season, I have faithfully lived by that principle of restoration. Staying focused on preparing myself for my future, and less focused on my obstacles, I gained strength to keep pushing forward to my imagined future, until I looked around and realized I was standing in it. My imagined future had become my 'present.' You can and will do the same. You will experience double (or even more) for your troubles. Trust God to heal your hurts, to handle your enemies, and to restore you completely.

| Key takeaway: |
| --- |
| Goal(s): |
| What will I stop? |
| What will I minimize? |
| What will I keep doing? |
| What will I do more of? |
| What will I start? |
| What is my timeline / deadline? |
| With what person(s) will I share these commitments? |

# Chapter 6

Are you using all of your available keys?

Knowledge is often right within our reach; and, when grasped, becomes a writ of passage – unlocks opportunity. That knowledge has a direct mandate for us and impact on our environments and outcomes. I reiterate this: there are many avenues from which we can gain knowledge. Sometimes we look past some of our greatest opportunities. Consider this: "The *right* question asked of the *right* person can unlock a treasure of knowledge for your life."

Do not overlook the knowledge immediately around you. Let us also concentrate on who is surrounding us, in our very midst, and what treasures are stored in the people we already know. Think about the times you had a conversation with someone, and you did not know what to say. Small talk, mindless conversation, is all you had to offer. This often happens with our close or extended familial relationships and people we interact with regularly. For another example, maybe you felt intimidated because someone was very accomplished, and you felt diminished in their presence, had a loss for words, or avoided speaking because you did not know what to say.

Let us be prepared for that next opportunity. Have the right questions. Strategically ask for the right opportunities to have those discussions on purpose. Everyone you know has something to offer – a treasure to unfold. We people all around who have unique skill sets and experiences, and we often are not aware of what they have accomplished, seen, or endured.

I will never forget that I had been in the field of human resources for 10 years before I ever took the opportunity to interview one of my aunts. While interviewing her, I learned something pivotal to my career.

The genesis of this conversation was my research for a speaking event called "Women Trailblazing in History." Instead of looking out further for women to admire during this nationally recognized month of celebration, I thought I would look closer to home. I had no idea what treasures would unfold. I was interviewing my aunt, who I had known for 40 years of my life at that time, and I had been in Human Resources (as my own career) for over 10 years by the time of this conversation. It was not until this interview that I discovered she had retired from my field, *human resources*, and she had blazed an incredible trail. At the peak of her career, she worked for one of the largest gas and oil companies in the world, pioneering as a woman (and first woman of color) in her role for the oil and gas industry. I had the privilege of asking questions such as 'what was it like,' 'what were the barriers and obstacles that you overcame,' and 'tell me the things that you learned and want to share with me.' Those were first-hand answers I would have never known. It changed me. It changed my life, my outlook, and how I saw myself in my profession.

I then realized there was someone who had come before me who had earned their way, against all odds, and I had no right to fail. Because the path had been cleared for me, and it was my job and my duty to walk that path and go beyond where she had gone. Because her *blood, sweat and tears* brought her through that journey, I do not have a right to fail or to back down from the things that she endured and already overcame. I realized that those obstacles were no longer truly in my way, and my mentality shifted. Because of her, I knew that I was an overcomer – more than an overcomer, a champion. Some of us will do even greater work than those who have come before us, because we are standing on their shoulders.

Sometimes we admire others, but we do not realize the baton is being passed to us. Our knowledge of where they have been, our knowledge of their accomplishments, their obstacles, their strategies that they used to overcome... those pieces of knowledge are our KEYS. Those are keys to unlock treasures in our own lives.

| |
|---|
| Key takeaway: |
| Goal(s): |
| What will I stop? |
| What will I minimize? |
| What will I keep doing? |
| What will I do more of? |
| What will I start? |
| What is my timeline / deadline? |
| With what person(s) will I share these commitments? |

# Chapter 7

Do you have 'something that nobody can take away?'

My late grandmother, as previously mentioned, shared those inspired words with me, while standing in the kitchen of her home where she single-handedly raised five children. Those words seem to have been imprinted on my soul: "Get something up there that can't nobody take away." She stated this as she pointed to her head. She was a *first*. As a girl, she was determined to graduate from high school, even during a time when young girls (including her, at the age of 9) often needed to stay home from school to babysit younger siblings, cook, and care for the house, while the older children and adults worked in the fields. Being a support to the home was emphasized more than education, because families needed everyone in the household contributing, just to make *ends meet*. Those circumstances did not stop Granny from getting her high school education, which she accomplished after most others in her area (by her age) had stopped going to school. Though she raised her children by providing cleaning services for a medical practice until retirement, her meticulousness, professionalism, and articulate manner of interacting with everyone endeared her to the doctor who employed her, as well as the staff. Undoubtedly, her sense of pride and work standards came from her academically enhanced ability to read and express, as well as from the tenacity she gained from learning how to *finish*. Her communication skills, along with her confident *spirit of excellence*, caused her and others to recognize her for more than her title – they saw what she had on the inside.

Knowledge can readily be gained from educational endeavors. It has become common to see people with self-proclaimed titles, but in the end, it takes discipline, study, and a desire to do what many are simply too lazy to do. However, if we do not have the education/credentials and credibility that are required for our field of interest, we may never receive the respect, favor and opportunities we desire or need. It is not only in the credentialing, but it is also in the competencies that are gained during the process of educational achievement. I encourage all to seek education, credentials, and skills for our trade, because the more knowledgeable we are about what we do, the more potential we have when our opportunity comes, and the more confidence we gain.

Like screwing a lightbulb into a socket, knowledge gives us the capacity for power. Having knowledge is like upgrading our engines. We can gather that knowledge even from those in our midst. When the ignition or the light switch of life opportunity is turned on, will we have the power and resources to engage? When opportunity comes, will we be ready?

Oftentimes, we gauge our progress through comparison to those around us, thinking 'if only we can be like them.' However, there are no copycats in life. Every fingerprint is unique and wonderful. We will glean from others, but we will not compare ourselves to others. We will multiply the knowledge they share by adding to that knowledge from our own life experiences, abilities and other resources.

We can take what we glean from others, and then add the latest technology, the latest skills, the latest strategies, and the latest processes for accomplishing our own unique dreams. The more knowledgeable we are, the more efficient and effective we can become in our fields. We are not learning just for the sake of education, but for the sake of enrichment. We are not merely consuming information or *enduring* an unenjoyable process. If we are simply enduring the process of education, then we are not getting the most out of it, and we are unlikely to recall or be changed by anything we have learned. That is not genuine education – that is not true enrichment. It is vitally important to find the *right* path to knowledge, and to enjoy the exploration – the journey. Most importantly – *take* the journey.

Again, what is the real impact of knowledge? For another analogy, knowledge very simply expands our framework. Imagine a blueprint. Think of knowledge as expanding that blueprint – adding square footage. Knowledge does not build the house, but it enlarges the territory. The *potential* for the building/house increases, as more knowledge is added (like expanding the blueprint).

The more knowledge we gain, however, the more we should also realize how much more we *do not* know. We should become aware of the vastness of space and journey 'beyond.' So, while knowledge expands us, it also should humble us. Knowledge should help us recognize that we *do not* know it all. The most ignorant person is one who believes they know everything about their field or about what they are doing. The wisest person may not be the most knowledgeable, but they have the framework for learning. They know where to find the knowledge, and they realize that they need to ask the right questions and do their own due diligence.

The awareness of *more* is the most important aspect of knowledge. In educating yourself, you realize how much you *do not* know. Yet, in educating yourself, you create a framework and ability to grow and achieve more, and you create the potential to become the very best at what you do – more importantly, to become the best version of yourself.

So, gain knowledge. Sure! Gain knowledge from educational resources. Gain knowledge from networks of communities and organizations, and from people in a related field. Networks are an excellent opportunity, because within networks are classes, workshops, and discussions. Gain knowledge from self-driven research and books. There are times when we are financially unable to go get a formal education, but that should not hinder us. Use the resources we *can* access.

We might be surprised at the opportunities that are opened when someone next to us or our supervisor finds out that we know *more*. Maybe we know more than what we are required to know for our current position, but we are faithful and do excellent work every day. Listen – it is only a matter of time before that pays off. When the right person learns of our potential, it creates opportunities for our advancement. *We* create the potential for promotion with knowledge, and *others* offer us the opportunity when the potential is recognized.

When preparation meets opportunity, it can be explosive. So, it is of utmost importance that we 'get something that nobody can take away.'

| |
|---|
| Key takeaway: |
| Goal(s): |
| What will I stop? |
| What will I minimize? |
| What will I keep doing? |
| What will I do more of? |
| What will I start? |
| What is my timeline / deadline? |
| With what person(s) will I share these commitments? |

# Conclusion

Are you ready to achieve your next level of success and influence?

Are you ready to break through barriers with internal growth?

Can you think outside of your current circumstances?

Can you imagine greater?

Are you willing to make the necessary adjustments?

Are you willing to take the limits off your own power?

Will you allow yourself to be healed and restored?

Lastly, will you increase your potential by adding knowledge from every available source, including those around you and by formal and informal education?

Your inner growth is the key to increasing your potential, and your potential is the key to being ready for the opportunities coming your way. Commit yourself to answering the tough questions. Commit yourself to the discipline of growth. Know within yourself that absolutely nothing can stop you from going to the next level, because growth is not about title or income as much as growth is about internal breakthrough.

# <u>Next in the Series:</u>

In this first book, Workforce Champion: Breaking Through, we addressed two principles: Imagining greater and the principle of inner growth. Next in the series, we will look at what winners do even when no one is watching. Please stay tuned for Workforce Champion: Behind Closed Doors.

# About the Author

LaTonya Darneish McElroy SPHR, SHRM-SCP has been in the field of Human Resources for over 16 years and considers Workforce Champion to be a God-inspired work of the heart.

It is her desire to inspire others to be champions in the workplace. Championing begins with internal growth and never ends. It is the work of continual development, humility, and reinvesting in the future, with the end-goal of creating a better self and to have a greater and more positive impact on our co-workers, our families, our businesses, and our communities.

Membership Affiliations:

Society for Human Resources Management (SHRM)

Texas State SHRM Council Volunteer

Tri-State SHRM Chapter

Jack & Jill of America, Inc.

Greater Texarkana Chamber of Commerce

Education, Hospital & Other Local Nonprofit Board Volunteer

Local Christian Church Leader and Volunteer

# Works Cited:

Nedergaard M, Goldman SA. BRAIN DRAIN. Scientific American. 2016 Mar;314(3):44-49. DOI: 10.1038/scientificamerican0316-44.

"Olive Tree." Olive Tree Bible Software, https://www.olivetree.com/.

Sasson, Remez. "Your Imagination Is Your Key to Success and Accomplishment." *Success Consciousness | Positive Thinking - Personal Development*, 4 July 2021, www.successconsciousness.com/blog/creative-visualization/imagination-is-your-key-to-success/.